# Wandering Wonderful

*poems by*

## Sarah Whiteley

*Finishing Line Press*
Georgetown, Kentucky

# Wandering Wonderful

## ACKNOWLEDGMENTS

My eternal gratitude to all those who support and inspire me, but most
especially to Kathleen Everett, Martin Shone, Leo LeBlanc, John & Dixie
Lehmann, Jonnie Kay Anderson, Mary Theiler, and James Whiteley.

Publisher: Leah Maines
Editor: Christen Kincaid
Cover Art: Sarah Whiteley
Author Photo: Sarah Whiteley
Cover Design: Leah Huete

Printed in the USA on acid-free paper.
Order online: www.finishinglinepress.com
also available on amazon.com

Author inquiries and mail orders:
Finishing Line Press
P. O. Box 1626
Georgetown, Kentucky 40324
U. S. A.

# Table of Contents

*for Charlie and porch beers and adventure…*

## early snow

an early snow this year

icy and hard, it woke me—
hissing and insistent
through the crack in the sill

the dogs both dig deeper
into my side, settle once more,
and sigh—little heart-furnaces

## winter talisman

I pulled on wool socks,
and world-weary shoes,
and walked through
the hushful early snow
seeking some small talisman

too late now for
the bright satisfaction
of a horse chestnut,
I settled instead
for the flakes falling white

through the luminous maple
still trembling red,
and for the dusting
of ice on the last
of the pale anemones

how I could swear I heard
the oaks sigh as I and the
weather passed by

## winter's arrival

even in cold weather,
I like the windows cracked

I can hear winter arrive then
and settle under the eaves,

chafing his gray hands
against the chill

the chickadees don't mind
how winter lurks there

so long as there is sun
and seed upon the sill

**juncos**

the juncos have not departed from the cold,
but instead have nested deep inside the camellia

with a full consideration of cones from the cedar
dropped within reach for hungry inspection

in the compulsory tedium of mid-winter,
their home will suddenly adorn itself in eddies of pink

and the juncos themselves, nut-shaded blossoms
winging between the leaves of winter's scree

## the winter wait

for everyone but the birds,
winter is about waiting

they must wonder why it is
we've seemingly stalled

piled on days of cold and rain
have made us slow and passive

and we miss seeing that
what is gray is also glistening

## altered dimensions

when the dogs grow tired—
much sooner now than before—

one stretched before the radiator,
the other with tail curled over nose

I worry about the change in space
coming from not too far away

how, dog-less, my dimensions will alter
the way in which they retain light

how the mind will still think to watch for
wagging shadows trailing at my heels

never far behind, regardless of absence

## funeral blouse

it could not be purely black,

though decency might
have said otherwise

but who would blame me
for wanting flowers the day of

for donning soft coppers split
by sprouts of old gold—

leaves and petals spread
outward and up,

plucking with quiet ease
a tear-sprigged heart

on a field of silken black

## plum trees

even at night the plum trees,
peppery sweet, cup the light

some eventual evening
a dogged wind will arrive,

sweep their pink pleats
off down the street,

our morning feet blessed
by the morsels it left

## plum plunder

half a dozen jays
are in the plum tree,
shrieking their delight
and coloring the walks
red beneath them
with dropped plunder

the dogs and I tip-toe
through their battlefield
but still come through with
sticky shoes, sticky paws,
and the cries of the flying
in our ears

**the purpose of a porch**

imperfection is precisely
what is called for—

the wood should creak
and weather,  flake
after the heavy, humid
days of summer

and an almost-slant can
change the perceptions
of porch dwellers,

lending a perhaps better view
of the net that light casts
over the horse chestnut

a good design stretches
lazy afternoon into deep twilight
stitched bright with fireflies
and tales we call friends

## summer crickets

prayer is a cricket—
whether one or many,

the point is the plea
on a summer's night

so hot and still the creek
becomes a motive,

a silvery enticement
sliding with delight

between banks rife
with lank grasses

teeming with the black gleam
of summer's invocation

## August at Olallie Lake

barely gray yet
and everything is still

the first shadows
crouch in waiting

while two coyotes sing
at the edge of the lake

first raven cleaves
the rising sky

the heart of the world
breaks open

and here is morning

## August, Highway 112

the owl lay on the side of the road
with a blue grace of lupines,

feather-tips stirred by passing cars,
they rose as if in recollection of flight—

that birthright of only the lightest bones

caught up in feather-envy,
I would have lingered longer

but felt an intruder upon death,
upon the remnants of a final flight

best left to the late summer grasses
grown high against the fence

and the wind just wandering through

## September at Shi Shi

like those stars above Shi Shi in September,
I thought I could not count them all—

there is no other desolation like reaching
the last of a thing before you realize it—

arriving at the lonely moment when the countless
has been counted after all

## autumn goodbye

November chill
rusts the dogwood,
scatters the locust seeds
down the sodden street

the maple this year
shows an unusual
reluctance for red
but today gray was made
a near beautiful thing –

a frame for the darker
darts of the chickadees
in the yellow goodbye
of the chestnut tree

**transitory**

the weightier light of November
cannot long sustain itself,

drifts lower sooner—
a season's gradual depletion

late season walks are divided among
vacant trees and roving leaves—

the perfect emptiness
for muted contemplation,

for palming small remembrances,
and partings mercifully labeled

*just for now*

## November vanishment

every November
when the wind comes
savage and dazzling
to undress the locust
of her autumn

I am startled
by the thousand
vanished yellows—
by sudden absence
after ferocious goodbye

## fog sounds

I love the fogs
of fall, everything
pulled nearer
except for sound—

which, muffled,
seems to say
there can be nothing
more important to hear
than silence just now

**uproarious**


to say that a landscape
can never be clamorous

disregards the wild
hearts within it,

forgets the crows
and casts no winds

an outlook is only
sometimes peaceful,

and mostly uproarious

**a piece of paradise**

quietly, I have tucked the woods
into a corner of myself, secure

so that waking, stretching,
I can smell the lake

can rise to the shades of hungry jays
seeking breakfast leftovers

I have gathered grasses
and countless wind-turned leaves

so that working, forgetting,
I can hear them hum

and lose a concrete hour
apart from high-rises

I have kept a piece a paradise
covert, concealed—

the final place to leave me,
the last place I depart

**cacophony**

such a cacophony of wrens
this morning as they collected
on my window sill

I could clearly hear them
through two solid inches
of closed pine door

all this joyous, feathered ruckus—
passing by in the hall, what
must the neighbors think?

## certainty in youth

when we were young together
and fairly crowded with belief,

certainty was a boat on the lake
our lines dropped and waiting

always there was the flourish of fish,
and the turtles sinking away from view,

and there still, the sprigs of wintergreen
beneath the waiting pines on the hill

## discernment

I stood, still as dropped stone,
to try and discern what it is
that the pines speak, so softly,
as the wind slips down the slope
to nightly greet them—

maybe because I could not
quiet my heart absolutely,
such discernment must remain
unknowable grace

### hiking near Mt Adams

every pine a prayer
for strength and sky,

these are surely temples
and I a clumsy guest
among soft-pawed congregants—

I walk reverent nonetheless

## finding away

when the light is just so and I am alone—
away from the meat of the world

when *remember* is a quiver of drab wings
and earth is absolution,

there is a drum the body holds that
when struck with perfect intention

sends thunder through feet

## an adjuration

those days that cannot be heard
above the rush of the river, that cannot
be heeded beyond the hail of the hawk
high in the cedar—embrace them

those days in which the woods
are committed only to wind, to sudden
falls of snow from the bending branches
of endless heights of pine

the days of peace unparalleled,
unfound inside of city-ordinary—
live them and then when they are gone,
unwind them, reel them back in,
and have them once again

## wandering wonderful

I'm pulling out the maps again—
it's been too long now
since I've gone in search of
nothing in particular

too long since I can say
I have delightedly stumbled upon
that perfect twist in a river
in the deep green of evening
somewhere in the middle
of maybe Montana

I'll always prefer them as paper—
I can unfold such a landscape,
smooth out the canyoned creases,
and fall back into wandering
wonderful, just as if I'd never left

## wind

wind is an old song

the cedar sings it
while others—

tired perhaps
of trying—

fall beneath it

become the curved
perches of ferns

**the rain in the locust**


last night, the rain
was the only thing playing,

sedately erasing building edges
and moon-ly margins—

nothing crisp, but the hiss
of the drops through the locust

**tree talk**

the sawara doesn't give up its secrets—
you have to come back again

and again let your hands ask of it
the same questions

and maybe stop by sometimes to see if
the copper beech has something new to say

one day, I found the blue feathers
of a Steller's jay lying under the cedar

likely the work of a hungry hawk,
though the wisps of bark were silent
on that question too

Sarah Whiteley is a Northwestern poet with Midwestern roots. Much of her work embodies her search for the innate beauty in small things and in the everyday workings of life. She currently lives high on a hill in Seattle with her two dogs, who she calls "the most perfect of companions." More of Sarah's poetry can be found on her blog at www.ebbtide.wordpress.com.

CPSIA information can be obtained
at www.ICGtesting.com
Printed in the USA
BVHW031441300519
549714BV00001B/123/P